YOUR PASSPORT TO
ECUADOR

by Sarah Cords

CONTENT CONSULTANT

Ernesto Capello, PhD
Professor of History and Latin
American Studies
Macalester College

CAPSTONE PRESS
a capstone imprint

Capstone Captivate is published by Capstone Press, an imprint of Capstone.
1710 Roe Crest Drive
North Mankato, Minnesota 56003
www.capstonepub.com

Library of Congress Cataloging-in-Publication Data
Names: Cords, Sarah Statz, 1974- author.
Title: Your passport to Ecuador / by Sarah Cords.
Description: North Mankato : Capstone Press, [2021] | Series: World
  passport | Includes index. | Audience: Grades 4-6
Identifiers: LCCN 2020001094 (print) | LCCN 2020001095 (ebook) | ISBN
  9781496684028 (hardcover) | ISBN 9781496687944 (paperback) | ISBN
  9781496684530 (pdf)
Subjects: LCSH: Ecuador--Description and travel--Juvenile literature. |
  Ecuador--Social life and customs--Juvenile literature.
Classification: LCC F3708.5 .C67 2020 (print) | LCC F3708.5 (ebook) | DDC
  986.6--dc23
LC record available at https://lccn.loc.gov/2020001094
LC ebook record available at https://lccn.loc.gov/2020001095

Image Credits
Alamy: Pere Rotger/Index/Heritage Image Partnership Ltd, 9; iStockphoto: 4FR, 16 (tortoise), Allan Watson, 21, DC_Colombia, cover (bottom); Newscom: Ballesteros/EFE, 12; Red Line Editorial: 5; Shutterstock Images: Abs Shrestha, 16 (seal), Agami Photo Agency, 16 (finch), Alejo Miranda, 19, betto rodrigues, 27, Brendan van Son, 6, Cao Romero, 22, Diego Grandi, 18, Ecuadorpostales, 11, Filip Bjorkman, cover (map), Fotos593, 15, Gil C, cover (flag), Guido Vermeulen-Perdaen, 16 (cormorant), Lukas Hodon, 28, Marek Poplawski, 7, Maridav, 16 (penguin), Neil Burton, 16 (iguana), nouseforname, 25, Ryan M. Bolton, 16 (lizard), Sidhe, 10, Terence Mendoza, 16 (locust)
Design Elements: iStockphoto, Shutterstock Images

Editorial Credits
Editor: Jamie Hudalla; Designer: Colleen McLaren

Printed in the United States of America.
PA117

CONTENTS

Words in **bold** are in the glossary.

CHAPTER ONE

WELCOME TO ECUADOR!

The Pacific Ocean laps against the shore of the Galápagos Islands. Crabs and lizards crawl on the sandy beaches. A giant tortoise rests on a rock. These reptiles can weigh nearly 1,000 pounds (454 kilograms) and live to be 150 years old! Many people travel to the islands to see this animal and others. The islands offer a variety of rare plants and animals.

The islands belong to Ecuador, a country on the northwestern coast of South America. People have lived on the land that is now Ecuador for thousands of years. Many cultures have shared the land. It was once a part of the **Inca Empire**. Spain also ruled the region.

MAP OF ECUADOR

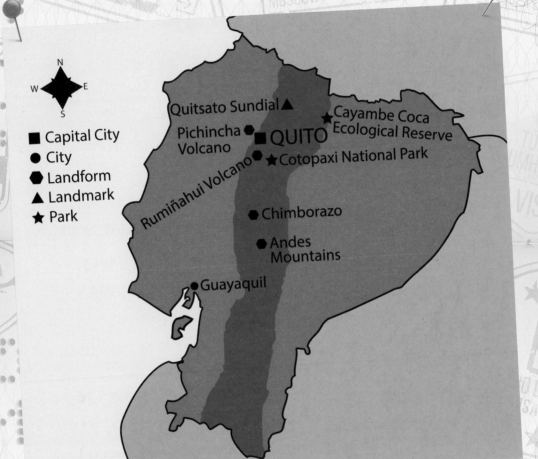

Capital City
City
Landform
Landmark
Park

Quitsato Sundial
Pichincha Volcano
QUITO
Cayambe Coca Ecological Reserve
Cotopaxi National Park
Rumiñahui Volcano
Chimborazo
Andes Mountains
Guayaquil

Explore Ecuador's cities and landmarks.

Sea lions nap on the sandy beaches of the Galápagos Islands.

PEOPLE AND CLIMATE

More than 16 million people live in Ecuador. Some work on farms, but most live in cities. More than 90 percent of people speak Spanish. Others speak a **native** language called Kichwa.

Ecuador is on the equator. The equator is an invisible line that divides Earth into its northern and southern halves. The country mainly experiences two seasons: wet and dry. The temperature is between 70 degrees Fahrenheit (21 degrees Celsius) and 80°F (27°C) all year. Because of the nice weather, people enjoy spending time in the beautiful natural areas. They also play outdoor sports such as soccer, which they call football.

Some people in Ecuador live along the beach.

FACT FILE

OFFICIAL NAME: .... THE REPUBLIC OF ECUADOR
POPULATION: 16,498,502
LAND AREA: .... 106,888 SQ. MI. (276,841 SQ KM)
CAPITAL: .... QUITO
MONEY: .... U.S. DOLLAR
GOVERNMENT: .... REPUBLIC, WITH AN ELECTED PRESIDENT
LANGUAGE: .... SPANISH AND KICHWA
GEOGRAPHY: Ecuador has different zones, including the Andes Mountains, tropical rain forests, beaches, and the Galápagos Islands. Peru and Colombia border Ecuador.
NATURAL RESOURCES: Ecuador has bananas, oil, fish, crabs, lobsters, and cocoa beans.

CHAPTER TWO

HISTORY OF ECUADOR

Groups of people in Ecuador have changed over the years. One of the earliest groups was the Valdivia. Some farmed and fished. Others made pottery bowls and jars.

The Valdivians lived in the area 5,500 years ago. They built their houses in a circle. The circle faced a public **plaza** where people could gather.

THE INCA EMPIRE

In the 1400s **CE**, Ecuador wasn't a country yet. Different groups of people split the area. In Cusco, a city in what is now Peru, the Inca Empire ruled. Around the year 1500, rulers of this empire moved into what is now Ecuador. People who already lived there fought against the empire. But the Inca won and took over the area.

Early groups of people in Ecuador made pottery figures.

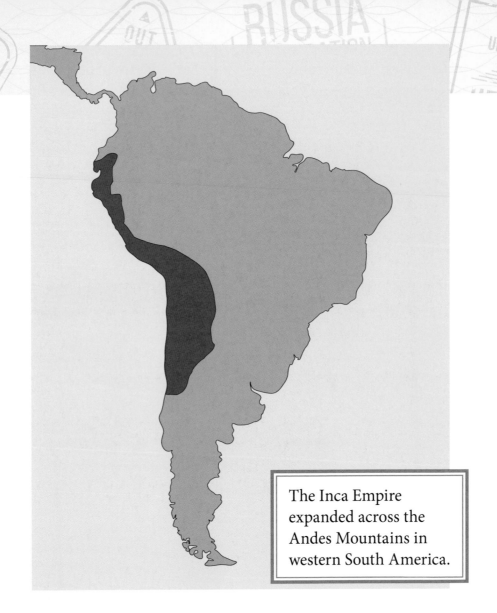

The Inca Empire expanded across the Andes Mountains in western South America.

SPANISH CONQUISTADORS

Soldiers called **conquistadors** arrived in Ecuador in the 1530s. They were from Spain. An Inca leader fought them. The Spanish killed him. Then one of the Inca leader's soldiers, Rumiñahui, fought the Spanish.

A volcano in Ecuador is named after Rumiñahui. The name means *rocky face.*

In 1534, Rumiñahui ordered the city of Quito to be destroyed. He wanted it gone so he wouldn't have to give it to the Spanish soldiers. The Spanish conquered the area. They began to rebuild Quito in 1534.

Before becoming president, Lenín Moreno was vice president from 2007–2013.

SPANISH COLONIAL RULE

Starting in the 1500s, Spain began colonizing parts of South America. From 1535 to 1822, Spain ruled Ecuador. Spain controlled Ecuador's money and treated the Spanish residents better than everyone else. The **indigenous** peoples of Ecuador grew frustrated with being poorly treated. In 1809, rebels in Quito declared **independence** from Spain. They were the first people in South America to declare independence. In 1822, Ecuador became an independent country. Now the country is a **republic** with a president. Presidents can serve up to eight years in office.

ECUADOR'S PRESIDENT

The head of state in Ecuador is the president. President Lenín Moreno was elected in 2017. He is one of the few world leaders to use a wheelchair.

CHAPTER THREE

EXPLORE ECUADOR

Ecuador is named after the equator. The equator runs through the middle of the planet. There are several sites to visit on the equator. One site is the Quitsato Sundial. It is a large instrument that tells time from the position of the sun in the sky. When the sun is directly overhead at noon, the sundial casts no shadow. People can also explore the Intiñan Solar Museum. Visitors go on tours and do science experiments set up by the museum. Many people also stop to take photographs by the Middle of the World monument. They can place one foot in the northern half and one foot in the southern.

THE GALÁPAGOS ISLANDS

The Galápagos Islands are 605 miles (1,000 km) off the coast of Ecuador. They consist of 13 major islands. They are a UNESCO World Heritage Site. These sites are important to everyone in the world.

Tourists can place one foot on each side of the equator at the Middle of the World monument.

ECUADOR 0°- 0'- 0" LAT.

RARE ANIMALS

BELOW ARE ANIMALS FOUND ONLY IN THE GALÁPAGOS ISLANDS

GALÁPAGOS TORTOISES

MARINE IGUANAS

LAVA LIZARDS

GALÁPAGOS FUR SEALS

GALÁPAGOS PENGUINS

FLIGHTLESS CORMORANTS

LARGE PAINTED LOCUSTS

DARWIN'S FINCHES

Some of the world's rarest animals, such as rainbow-colored iguanas and blue-footed birds, live on the Galápagos Islands. One fish even looks like a bat!

MOUNTAINS AND VOLCANOES

In the center of the country are the Andes Mountains. Two different ridges of this mountain range run side by side. The entire area is called the Andes Highlands, or the Sierra. Many volcanoes can be found here. This area is a part of the Ring of Fire, an active trail of volcanoes along the Pacific Ocean.

FACT

There are more than 40 volcanoes in Ecuador and the Galápagos Islands. One volcano, Chimborazo, is the highest mountain in Ecuador. It is also the farthest distance on the planet from the center of Earth.

CENTURIES-OLD CITIES

Quito, Ecuador's capital, is a very old city. A famous section of the city is called Old Town. Many of its beautiful churches were built in the 1700s.

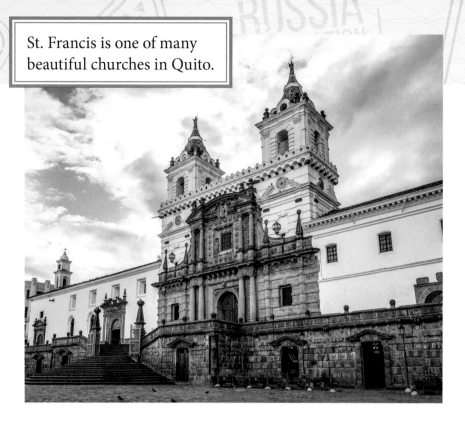

St. Francis is one of many beautiful churches in Quito.

Quito is high in the Andes Mountains under the Pichincha volcano. More than 1.5 million people live there. It is a UNESCO World Heritage Site.

People pack the streets of Guayaquil, Ecuador's largest city. About 2.3 million people live there. Located on the country's southern coast, it is a major **port**. Most of Ecuador's **exports** are put on ships in Guayaquil. Then they are sent to the rest of the world. Visitors can discover history museums in Guayaquil. Presley Norton Museum contains items made by the ancient Valdivians.

Limpiopungo Lake and the volcano Cotopaxi are in Cotopaxi National Park.

BEAUTIFUL NATURAL AREAS

One of the most exciting parks in Ecuador is Cotopaxi National Park. It has an active volcano. Visitors hike and bike in the park. People also enjoy the Cayambe Coca Ecological Reserve. This park has the tallest waterfall in Ecuador.

CHAPTER FOUR

DAILY LIFE

Family life is very important in Ecuador. Families host quinceañera parties to celebrate when girls turn 15. Young people often live with their parents even when they attend college. Family members, including grandparents and cousins, typically live close together.

MANY LANGUAGES

Most Ecuadorians speak Spanish. But that is not the only language spoken there. Another popular local language is Kichwa. Schools in Ecuador offer a **bilingual** education. They have classes in both Spanish and indigenous languages. Kids in Ecuador usually start school around age 6. Education is free through college.

FACT

In mountain communities, people often wear ponchos. Ponchos keep people warm and dry.

Multiple generations of a family often live together.

Plantain chips are often served as a side dish.

COMMON MEALS

Ecuador has many farms. Farmers grow many crops, including plantains. Plantains are a type of banana that is usually cooked. Ecuador exports more bananas around the world than any other country!

PEOPLE OF ECUADOR

The majority of people who live in Ecuador are *mestizo*. They have both indigenous and European ancestors. Another group of people are known as the Montubio. They first lived on the coast of Ecuador. Other indigenous peoples include the Kichwa and the Shuar.

Various soups are popular in Ecuador. Soups are sometimes made using fish. They are often very spicy. Ecuadorians make empanadas, which are small meat pies. People also like llapingachos. These are pancakes made from mashed potatoes. They are often stuffed with cheese.

PLANTAIN CHIPS

About 10 percent of the world's bananas are grown in Ecuador. That's about 6.6 million tons (6 million metric tons)! People in Ecuador enjoy cooking one type of banana called a plantain. With the help of an adult, you can make plantain chips at home.

Ingredients:
- 4 plantains
- 3–4 tablespoons of olive oil
- Sea salt

Plantain Directions:

1. Preheat oven to 400°F.
2. Peel plantains. Slice plantains very thin.
3. Toss slices in olive oil.
4. Lay out the slices on aluminum foil covering a cookie sheet.
5. Bake at 400°F for 17–20 minutes. They should be golden, but not too brown.
6. Take out of oven and let cool.
7. Lightly salt the slices.

CHAPTER FIVE

HOLIDAYS AND CELEBRATIONS

Some holidays in Ecuador are colorful displays of pride. The entire nation celebrates Independence Day on August 10. August 10 is the day Quito declared independence from Spain in 1822. There are parades and fairs. People go to concerts. They enjoy traditional folk dances.

RELIGIOUS CELEBRATIONS

A lot of Ecuadorians follow the Roman Catholic religion. In the spring they celebrate Easter. Before Easter, there is a time called Lent. It lasts for 40 days. Catholics make small sacrifices by giving up certain foods, such as meat. Before Lent is Carnival, usually in February or March. During Carnival, Ecuadorians march in parades. They toss colored flour on each other. This activity originated with the indigenous practice of throwing flowers during celebrations.

Dancers put on performances during Carnival.

REGIONAL CELEBRATIONS

Many regions of Ecuador have their own holidays. At the end of August, the Yamor Festival is held in Otavalo. People celebrate farming and corn planting. There are parades. People dance and enjoy music. There is also a swimming race in nearby San Pablo Lake.

FACT

People celebrate Carnival with huge water balloon fights.

CHAPTER SIX

SPORTS AND RECREATION

Soccer, or football, is very popular in Ecuador. There are 14 teams in its top national league. The Liga Deportiva Universitaria team from Quito played in the 2008 FIFA Club World Cup. This is the biggest championship in professional international soccer. They did not win, but they were the runners-up.

When athletes from Ecuador play games in Ecuador, they have a unique advantage. Ecuador is very mountainous. It is at a high altitude. The air is thinner there than at low altitudes. Team members from other countries have to work harder just to breathe. But athletes who are from Ecuador are used to the air. They don't get tired as quickly as their opponents.

Antonio Valencia is one of Ecuador's best football players.

Ecuador is a good place to hike because it is a mountainous country.

A VARIETY OF ACTIVITIES

Another popular sport in Ecuador is paddle ball. The game is played with a soft ball. Players use paddles to hit the ball back and forth.

There are also many places for Ecuadorians to enjoy mountain climbing. Two mountain ranges in Ecuador contain high peaks. Visitors who climb these mountains have awesome views.

From fiery volcanoes to colorful cities, Ecuador has sites everyone can enjoy. Its warm weather and outdoor activities make it a great place to explore and live.

ECUAVOLEY

Ecuavoley is a sport similar to volleyball. The game is popular in Ecuador—especially in the city of Quito. Ecuadorians invented it near the end of the 1800s. To play, you will need six people, a soccer ball, and a net.

1. Three players stand on each side of the net. Determine who will be the setter, the server, and the flyer.
2. The server starts by tossing the ball over the net to the other team.
3. The setter and flyer take turns keeping the ball off the ground and hitting it to the other team. Teams score a point when the ball hits the ground on the other team's side.
4. A set consists of 15 points. The game is played until one team wins two sets.

GLOSSARY

**bilingual
(bye-LING-gwuhl)**
able to speak two languages

CE
CE means Common Era, or after year one

**conquistadors
(kon-KEYS-tuh-dors)**
16th-century military leaders from Spain

exports (EK-sports)
products a country sells and ships to other countries

**Inca Empire
(EENG-kuh EM-pire)**
ruling empire in parts of Latin and South America from the 1400s to 1532

**independence
(in-di-PEN-duhns)**
the freedom a country has to govern itself

**indigenous
(in-DIJ-uh-nuhs)**
first people, plants, and animals to live in a country

native (NAY-tuhv)
born in a particular country or place; also, tied to a certain location

plaza (PLAZ-uh)
an open area where people can gather

port (PORT)
a place where ships are loaded and unloaded

republic (ri-PUHB-lik)
a type of government where people elect their political leaders and president

READ MORE

Boone, Mary. *Let's Look at Ecuador*. North Mankato, MN: Capstone Press, 2020.

Markovics, Joyce L. *Ecuador*. New York: Bearport Publishing, 2017.

Stine, Megan. *Where Are the Galapagos Islands?* New York: Grosset & Dunlap, 2017.

INTERNET SITES

DK Find Out!: Incas
https://www.dkfindout.com/us/history/incas

National Geographic Kids: Ecuador
https://kids.nationalgeographic.com/explore/countries/ecuador

Wonderopolis: Where Are the Galápagos Islands?
https://www.wonderopolis.org/wonder/where-are-the-galapagos-islands

INDEX

OTHER BOOKS IN THIS SERIES

YOUR PASSPORT TO CHINA
YOUR PASSPORT TO EL SALVADOR
YOUR PASSPORT TO ETHIOPIA
YOUR PASSPORT TO FRANCE
YOUR PASSPORT TO IRAN
YOUR PASSPORT TO KENYA
YOUR PASSPORT TO PERU
YOUR PASSPORT TO RUSSIA
YOUR PASSPORT TO SPAIN